D0700189

THE BEST
SOCCER
PLAYERS
OF ALL TIME

By Chrös McDougall

www.abdopublishing.com

Published by Abdo Publishing, a division of ABDO, PO Box 398166, Minneapolis, Minnesota 55439. Copyright © 2015 by Abdo Consulting Group, Inc. International copyrights reserved in all countries. No part of this book may be reproduced in any form without written permission from the publisher. SportsZone™ is a trademark and logo of Abdo Publishing.

Printed in the United States of America, North Mankato, Minnesota
092014
012015

THIS BOOK CONTAINS
RECYCLED MATERIALS

Cover Photos: Thanassis Stavrakis/AP Images, foreground; Richard Drew/AP Images, background
Interior Photos: Thanassis Stavrakis/AP Images, 1 (foreground); Richard Drew/AP Images, 1 (background); AP Images, 7, 9, 15, 17, 19, 21, 25, 29; Bippa/AP Images, 11, 13; Staff/AFP/Getty Images, 23; Carlo Fumagalli/AP Images, 27, 33; El Grafico/AP Images, 31; Abedin Taherkenareh/EPA/Newscom, 35; Luca Bruno/AP Images, 37; Lawrence Jackson/AP Images, 39; George Tiedemann/ZUMA Press/Newscom, 41; Eoghan McNally/Shutterstock Images, 43; Gouhier-Hahn-Orban/MCT/Newscom, 45; Cesar Rangel/AP Images, 47; Armando Franca/AP Images, 49; Marcio Jose Sanchez/AP Images, 51; Volker Hartmann/AP Images, 53; Petr David Josek/AP Images, 55; Greg Baker/AP Images, 57; AGIF/Shutterstock Images, 59; Christian Bertrand/Shutterstock Images, 61

Editor: Patrick Donnelly
Series Designer: Christa Schneider

Library of Congress Control Number: 2014944194

Cataloging-in-Publication Data
McDougall, Chrös.
 The best soccer players of all time / Chrös McDougall.
  p. cm. -- (Sports' best ever)
ISBN 978-1-62403-621-7 (lib. bdg.)
Includes bibliographical references and index.
1. Soccer--Juvenile literature.   I. Title.
796.334--dc23

                          2014944194

TABLE OF CONTENTS

INTRODUCTION

Some call soccer "the beautiful game."

For 90 minutes, the play rarely stops. Players are free to move around the field as they see fit. And when everything comes together for a goal, it's a magical moment.

The best players race around the field as if the ball is glued to their feet. They can beat defenders with cunning footwork and score with rocket shots. The best players must be smart and creative. They must have great vision, instincts, and confidence. And they must ultimately have great fitness. The average soccer player runs 7 miles (11.3 km) over a 90-minute game.

Here are some of the greatest players in soccer history.

ALFREDO DI STÉFANO

Real Madrid was on its way to the wrong side of history. It was 1956. The Spanish soccer club had reached the final of the first European Cup. But Real Madrid was trailing Stade de Reims of France 2–0 after just 10 minutes.

Then Alfredo di Stéfano made his move. The speedy forward raced into the top of the penalty box. In a flash, he received a pass and touched it into space. Then, before two defenders could close in, he drove a right-footed shot to the back of the net. That was the start of a comeback. Real Madrid eventually won 4–3.

Di Stéfano had a knack for winning. He won two league titles with River Plate in his native Argentina. Then he won four Colombian league titles in five years with Millonarios. It was with Real Madrid that di Stéfano became a legend, though.

Alfredo di Stéfano makes a play on the ball in 1963.

The team was not yet a power when he arrived in 1953. Then, in 11 seasons with di Stéfano, it won eight Spanish league titles. More importantly, it won the first five European Cups (now called Champions League). Di Stéfano, who scored in all five finals, was the team's leader and star throughout.

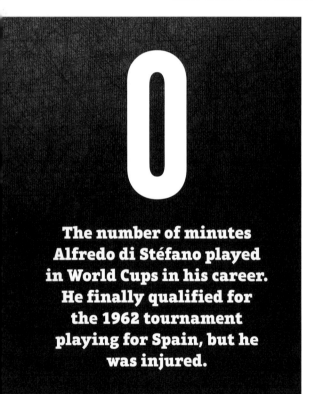

0

The number of minutes Alfredo di Stéfano played in World Cups in his career. He finally qualified for the 1962 tournament playing for Spain, but he was injured.

Di Stéfano was a dominant striker. He scored 418 goals in 510 games for Real Madrid. But "The Blond Arrow" was much more than that. Many consider him to be the game's most complete player of all time. Di Stéfano had great ball control with both his feet and his head. Plus he was fast and versatile enough to play all over the field, even on defense.

"He's the best I ever saw," said legendary England defender Bobby Charlton.

Alfredo di Stéfano, *far right*, scores a goal for Real Madrid in the 1960 European Cup Final.

ALFREDO DI STÉFANO

Position: Forward

Hometown: Buenos Aires, Argentina

Birth Date: July 4, 1926

National Teams: Argentina (1947), Spain (1957–61)

World Cup: 1962 (injured–did not play)

Pro Career: 1949–66

Club Teams: River Plate (Argentina), 1945, 1947–49; Huracán (Argentina), 1946; Millonarios (Colombia), 1949–52; Real Madrid (Spain), 1953–64; Espanyol (Spain), 1964–66

European Player of the Year: 1957, 1959

LEV YASHIN

No goalie likes to give up goals. But Lev Yashin *really* hated letting one slip past. So the Soviet goalkeeper did everything in his power to stop the ball.

Before Yashin, most goalies stayed on the goal line and let the action play out in front of them. Yashin made sure he was impossible to miss. In his trademark black uniform, "The Black Spider" covered the net as if he had eight legs. The 6-foot-3 keeper was known to burst off his line to knock away crosses when needed. And his voice was a constant presence directing his teammates from the back. Yashin set the standard most goalies today follow. But in his era, he was one of a kind. Yashin backstopped the golden era of Soviet soccer. With him in net, the Soviet Union won the 1956 Olympic gold medal and the 1960 European Championship.

Lev Yashin makes a diving stop against Germany in the 1966 World Cup semifinals.

The goalie's star shone brightest in his three World Cups, though.

The 1958 World Cup was the first to be broadcast on international TV. Fans were drawn to the charismatic Black Spider. His great confidence and reflexes in goal helped the Soviets reach the quarterfinals that year and in 1962. Then they finished fourth in 1966. No Russian or Soviet team had finished better through 2014.

Yashin's international success naturally drew interest from other club teams. But the goalie remained loyal to Dinamo Moscow for his entire 22-year career.

In 1963, Yashin was named the European Player of the Year. That award merged with the World Player of the Year Award in 2010. Yet through 2014, no other goalie had won the honor. It is a fitting distinction for the most unique of goalkeepers.

150

The estimated number of penalty shots Lev Yashin stopped during his career.

Lev Yashin was known for his acrobatic saves, like this one
in a win over Italy in the 1966 World Cup.

LEV YASHIN

Position: Goalkeeper
Hometown: Moscow, Russia
Birth Date: October 22, 1929
National Team: Soviet Union (1954–70)
World Cups: 1958, 1962, 1966, 1970
Pro Career: 1953–71
Club Team: Dinamo Moscow (Soviet Union), 1953–71
European Player of the Year: 1963

PELÉ

Pelé enjoyed a great start with his national team. At age 17, he led Brazil to its first World Cup title in 1958. He scored a hat trick in the semifinals and two goals in the final. But the great Brazilian goal scorer was injured during the 1962 World Cup. So he had to watch as teammate Garrincha led the team to victory.

Then came the 1966 World Cup. Opponents needed a way to stop the athletic and creative Pelé. So they set out to hurt him. It worked. Pelé missed the second game with an injury. And Brazil was eliminated in the group stage. Pelé said he was done with the World Cup after that.

Most soccer fans are happy that Pelé changed his mind. The 29-year-old Pelé joined the Brazil national team for one more World Cup in 1970. And it turned out to be the most memorable one yet.

Pelé is carried off the field by his teammates after Brazil's victory in the 1970 World Cup final.

That year's event in Mexico was the first broadcast on color TV. Fans were rewarded with perhaps the greatest team ever. Brazil combined amazing attacking flair with great discipline and organization. At the heart of the team was Pelé. He scored four goals, including one in the final, as Brazil won its third World Cup.

The win made Pelé a legend. His 12 World Cup goals were a record. So were his three championships. And his popularity continued to grow. Since 1956, Pelé had played with just one club team: Santos in Brazil. He retired in 1974. But in 1975 he joined the New York Cosmos in the North American Soccer League. Soccer was not very popular in the United States. But huge crowds came out to see the iconic player. When Pelé finally retired in 1977, he had 1,281 goals in 1,363 games. No player has since come close.

2

The number of days warring sides in Nigeria called a truce so they could watch Pelé play a 1967 friendly in that country.

Pelé shows perfect form on a bicycle kick in 1966.

PELÉ (EDSON ARANTES DO NASCIMENTO)

Position: Forward

Hometown: Tres Coracoes, Brazil

Birth Date: October 23, 1940

National Team: Brazil (1957–71)

World Cups: 1958 (win), 1962 (win), 1966, 1970 (win)

Pro Career: 1956–74, 1975–77

Club Teams: Santos (Brazil), 1956–74; New York Cosmos (USA), 1975–77

World Cup Honors: Golden Ball (best player), 1970; Silver Ball, 1958

17

FRANZ BECKENBAUER

When Franz Beckenbauer stepped onto the field, he took charge. The West Germany star known as "Der Kaiser" (The Emperor) was a leader. But he was also an innovator and a world-class talent.

Beckenbauer is most famous for his performance at the 1974 World Cup. He had previously led his team to a runner-up finish in 1966 and a third-place finish in 1970. But the 1974 tournament was held on home soil in West Germany. And this time, Beckenbauer was the team captain.

Originally a midfielder, Beckenbauer later became a shutdown defender. But by 1974, he was playing a revolutionary new role as sweeper. While on defense, he positioned himself in the back and organized the West Germany defense. But when his team attacked, Beckenbauer went too. This playing style was unique—and devastating.

Franz Beckenbauer hoists the World Cup trophy after West Germany's victory on home soil in 1974.

Beckenbauer played with an attacking flair not typical among German players. And his play helped West Germany defeat the dominant Netherlands 2–1 in the hotly anticipated 1974 final.

The 1974 World Cup was one of many highlights for "Der Kaiser." He debuted for Bayern Munich in 1964. The team was in the second division of the German league at the time. One decade later, Beckenbauer led the team to three straight European Cups from 1974 to 1976. From 1972 to 1976, he was twice named European Player of the Year and twice the runner-up. Later, he went to the United States and helped the New York Cosmos win three championships in four seasons.

In 1990, Beckenbauer once again lifted the World Cup trophy. This time he was manager of West Germany. "Der Kaiser" reigned again.

103

Franz Beckenbauer's caps with West Germany. He became the first player to appear in more than 100 games for the country.

Franz Beckenbauer, *left*, went on to star for the New York Cosmos after his brilliant European career.

FRANZ BECKENBAUER

Position: Sweeper

Hometown: Munich, Germany

Birth Date: September 11, 1945

National Team: West Germany (1965–77)

World Cups: 1966, 1970, 1974 (win)

Pro Career: 1964–82

Club Teams: Bayern Munich (West Germany), 1964–1977; New York Cosmos (USA), 1977–80, 1983; Hamburg (West Germany), 1980–82

World Cup Honors: Silver Ball, 1974

European Player of the Year: 1972, 1976

JOHAN
CRUYFF

Something interesting was brewing in Amsterdam, Netherlands, during the late 1960s. The club team Ajax was developing a new style of soccer. The players trained to be versatile. They could switch positions on a whim. And their tactics changed to fit the moment. The style was called "Total Football." And the man at the center of it was Johan Cruyff.

Officially, Cruyff was labeled a forward. On the field, though, he played everywhere. Cruyff could be a lethal striker. He could step back and be a playmaker. Or he could move to the wing and fool defenders with his famous "Cruyff turn." He would fake a pass or shot. Then he would drag the ball behind his planted foot, turn 180 degrees, and move into open space.

Johan Cruyff was known for his deft footwork that kept the ball away from defenders.

Cruyff excelled in all areas of the game. Ajax won six Dutch titles with Cruyff from 1966 to 1973. It won the European Cup in each of those last three years as well. Plus, Cruyff was named European Player of the Year in 1971 and 1973. He again won the award in 1974 after joining Barcelona in Spain.

Despite his talent, Cruyff never won a major international title. He came close, though. Total Football had spread to the Dutch national team by the 1974 World Cup. Through six games, the team had scored 14 goals and given up one. Cruyff then drew a penalty in the final. A teammate scored to put the Dutch up 1–0. But West Germany came back to win 2–1. Cruyff retired from the Dutch team before the 1978 tournament.

Cruyff played professionally until 1984. He then came back and had more success as a manager. In 1992, he led Barcelona to its first European Cup.

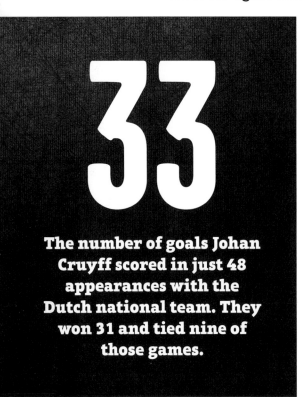

33

The number of goals Johan Cruyff scored in just 48 appearances with the Dutch national team. They won 31 and tied nine of those games.

Johan Cruyff blasts home a goal against Brazil in the 1974 World Cup semifinals.

JOHAN CRUYFF

Position: Center forward

Hometown: Amsterdam, Netherlands

Birth Date: April 25, 1947

National Team: Netherlands (1966–77)

World Cup: 1974

Pro Career: 1964–84

Club Teams: Ajax (Netherlands), 1964–73, 1981–83; Barcelona (Spain), 1973–78; Los Angeles Aztecs (USA), 1979; Washington Diplomats (USA), 1980–81; Levante (Spain), 1981; Feyenoord (Netherlands), 1983–84

World Cup Honors: Golden Ball, 1974

European Player of the Year: 1971, 1973, 1974

MICHEL PLATINI

The ball was a gift. From a broken play, it sat alone at the top of the penalty box. That is when Michel Platini pounced. His right-footed strike deflected off a defender. And the Danish goalkeeper did not have a chance. The 78th-minute goal gave Platini's France a 1–0 victory. And the 1984 European Championship on home soil had only just begun.

Platini scored nine goals over the course of five games. Twice he scored hat tricks. He scored with his left foot, his right foot, and his head. In an epic back-and-forth semifinal against Portugal, he scored the game winner with a minute to play in extra time. In the final, he scored on a free kick.

Put simply, Platini was brilliant. And his play led the stylish French team to its first victory in a major tournament.

Michel Platini leads the French team against Denmark in the 1984 European Championship.

France fans got used to Platini's magnificence during the 1970s and 1980s. The attacking midfielder blended amazing ball skills with a playmaker's vision and an eye for the goal. That made him the maestro of a world-class midfield known as "The Magic Square."

Platini was at the peak of his powers at the 1984 European Championship. The tournament came in the middle of his three consecutive European Player of the Year Awards. One year later, he led Juventus of Italy to the European Cup.

France would have to wait for its first World Cup victory. But Platini guided the squad to the 1982 and 1986 semifinals. Nobody questioned his place among the game's all-time greats after that. Upon retiring, Platini served as a coach. In 2007, he was voted president of the European soccer governing body.

41

The number of goals Michel Platini scored in 72 appearances for France, a team record at the time.

Michel Platini, *right*, takes on two Spanish defenders in the 1984 European Championship final.

MICHEL PLATINI

Position: Midfielder

Hometown: Joeuf, France

Birth Date: June 21, 1955

National Team: France (1976–1987)

World Cups: 1978, 1982, 1986

Pro Career: 1972–87

Club Teams: Nancy-Lorraine (France), 1972–79; Saint-Etienne (France), 1979–82; Juventus (Italy), 1982–87

European Player of the Year: 1983, 1984, 1985

DIEGO MARADONA

A miskicked clearing attempt floated through the penalty box toward England goalie Peter Shilton. But Diego Maradona, a wily 5-foot-5 forward for Argentina, reached the ball first. Maradona did not hit the ball with his head. Instead, he sneakily touched it with his left hand. The referees did not notice that, though. They only noticed the ball bouncing into the net.

The "Hand of God" was one of the most controversial goals in World Cup history. But it was not Maradona's only legacy from that 1986 World Cup quarterfinal match. Just three minutes later, he scored the "Goal of the Century." And there was no controversy about that one.

Maradona received a pass just short of midfield. In only three touches, he escaped two defenders and was off down the right sideline.

Diego Maradona, *left*, scores his infamous "Hand of God" goal against England in the 1986 World Cup.

Maradona cut past a defender. And just outside the penalty box, he cut to the outside past another one. Just before being taken down at the 6-yard box, Maradona slid the ball across the goal line.

The two goals gave Argentina a 2–1 win over England. A few days later, Argentina won its second World Cup title.

Maradona used his smaller size to his advantage. He could charge past opponents like a bull. Or he could use his footwork to dance around them like a ballerina. Yet he was a master playmaker as well. At his best, Maradona might have been the greatest ever. But he was also controversial. Maradona was outspoken and rebellious. He struggled with drug abuse and a wild lifestyle too. In fact, he was kicked out of the 1994 World Cup for failing a drug test. On the field, however, he was one of a kind.

53

The number of fouls committed against Diego Maradona during the 1986 World Cup, a record.

Diego Maradona is carried off the field, trophy in hand, after leading Argentina to the 1986 World Cup title.

DIEGO MARADONA

Position: Forward

Hometown: Buenos Aires, Argentina

Birth Date: October 30, 1960

National Team: Argentina (1974–94)

World Cups: 1982, 1986 (win), 1990, 1994

Pro Career: 1976–94, 1995–97

Club Teams: Argentinos Juniors (Argentina), 1976–81; Boca Juniors (Argentina), 1981–82, 1995–97; Barcelona (Spain), 1982–84; Napoli (Italy), 1984–91; Sevilla (Spain), 1992–93; Newell's Old Boys (Argentina), 1993–94

World Cup Honors: Golden Ball, 1986; Bronze Ball, 1990

PAOLO MALDINI

On January 20, 1985, a 16-year-old defender made his AC Milan debut as a halftime substitute. More than 24 years later, in 2009, Paolo Maldini finally retired at age 41. Maldini played in 902 games as a professional. And in all 902, he was wearing the red and black colors of AC Milan.

Maldini was known for his humility and gentlemanly play. But Maldini was also a winner. Perhaps no player has achieved more at the club level. Maldini helped Milan win seven Italian championships. He also guided the club to five Champions League titles. Only one player had won more through 2014.

Maldini actually joined AC Milan's youth program as a 10-year-old. His dad, Cesare Maldini, had been a star for AC Milan and Italy. Some thought the younger Maldini received special treatment due to his family name.

Paolo Maldini was a star for AC Milan for more than 24 years.

But Paolo quickly proved himself on the first team. He was a regular player by his second season. And in 1997, he took the captain's armband.

The sturdy defender played much of his career as a left back. However, he later moved to central defense. In both positions, he thrived. Maldini could play the ball strongly off either foot. Plus he had great speed, instincts, positioning, and tactical judgment. In a country known for great defenders, Maldini stood out for nearly a quarter century.

Maldini played 126 games for Italy. That was a team record. His teams were runners-up at the 1994 World Cup and the 2000 European Championship. However, he never won a major championship with the national team.

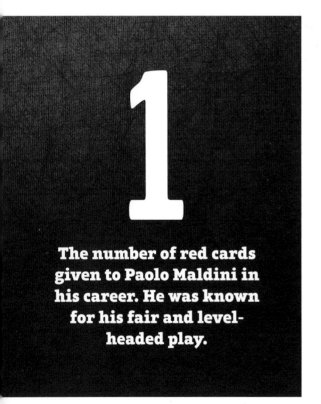

1

The number of red cards given to Paolo Maldini in his career. He was known for his fair and level-headed play.

Paolo Maldini makes an overhead kick for Italy against Czechoslovakia in the 1996 European Championship.

PAOLO MALDINI

Position: Defender
Hometown: Milan, Italy
Birth Date: June 26, 1968
National Team: Italy (1988–2002)
World Cups: 1990, 1994, 1998, 2002
Pro Career: 1984–2009
Club Team: AC Milan (Italy), 1984–2009

MIA
HAMM

Girls did not dream of playing for the US women's soccer team when Mia Hamm was born in 1972. That is because the team did not exist until 1985. Hamm debuted on that team two years later. And over the next 17 years, she gave a generation of girls something to strive for.

A tireless worker, Hamm became the most lethal scorer in women's soccer. And she could just as easily set up her teammates for goals. Her success with the national team helped elevate women's soccer to new heights. And by the time she retired in 2004, she was the iconic female athlete of her generation.

Hamm was just 15 years old when she first played for the United States. Few even knew the national team existed for its first decade. But Hamm quietly developed into the dominant player in the sport.

Mia Hamm leaps into the arms of Abby Wambach after scoring a goal for the Washington Freedom in 2003.

She was fast and had great ball control. But her trademark was her killer instinct around the goal. The goals and assists piled up. So did the hardware. Hamm helped the US team win the first Women's World Cup in 1991. Then she helped the team win the sport's first Olympic gold medal in 1996.

Nothing compared to the 1999 Women's World Cup, though. Huge crowds cheered the US team to victory on home soil. And much of the attention focused on the personable and potent Hamm.

Hamm ended her career with 158 international goals. She also had 144 assists. Those were easily world records. In addition to her two Women's World Cups, Hamm also won two Olympic gold medals. Her impact went beyond the numbers, though. Hamm's skills and charisma helped women's soccer grow to new heights.

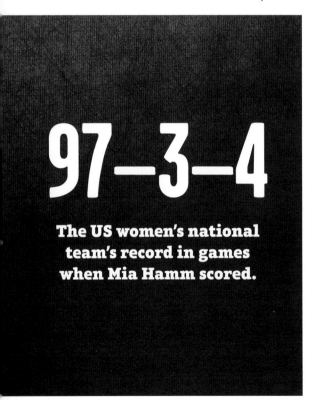

97–3–4

The US women's national team's record in games when Mia Hamm scored.

Mia Hamm zeroes in on the ball in the 2004 Olympics against Brazil.

MIA HAMM

Position: Forward

Hometown: Selma, Alabama

Birth Date: March 17, 1972

College: University of North Carolina

National Team: USA (1987–2004)

Women's World Cups: 1991 (win), 1995, 1999 (win), 2003

Olympic Games: 1996 (gold), 2000, 2004 (gold)

Club Team: Washington Freedom (USA), 2001–03

World Player of the Year: 2001, 2002*
*The women's award began in 2001

ZINEDINE ZIDANE

The 1998 World Cup was in France. After a shaky start, star French midfielder Zinedine Zidane got better with each round. But heading into the final against Brazil, he had yet to score a goal.

That finally changed in the 27th minute. On a corner kick, Zidane leaped above a defender and drilled a goal with his head. Just before halftime, he did it again. Zidane's two header goals led France to a 3–0 win over the defending champions. As the team's star, it was fitting for Zidane to be the one to lead France to its first World Cup. Yet it was a surprise that he did so with his head.

Zidane was methodical with the ball at his feet. His dribbling skills could mesmerize opponents. And his passes could find spots only he could see. These masterful skills and instincts were honed as a child playing on the streets of Marseille, France.

Zinedine Zidane was a longtime star for the French national team.

The player nicknamed "Zizou" had incredible highs in his career. He led France to victory at the 1998 World Cup and the 2002 European Championship. In 2002, his powerful left-footed volley from the top of the penalty box secured the Champions League title for Real Madrid. Zidane also won three World Player of the Year Awards.

But there were lows too. France performed poorly at the 2002 World Cup and the 2004 European Championship. Then Zidane began his final tournament, the 2006 World Cup, playing poorly. Yet the Zizou of old returned for the knockout round. His dominant play led France all the way back to the final.

However, Zidane's final play was a red card. He head-butted an opponent during the second extra-time period. Zidane still won the Golden Ball. But Italy won the World Cup in a shootout.

$65 million

The then-record transfer fee Real Madrid paid in 2001 to obtain Zinedine Zidane from Juventus.

Zinedine Zidane scores on a penalty kick against Portugal in the 2006 World Cup semifinals.

ZINEDINE ZIDANE

Position: Midfielder

Hometown: Marseille, France

Birth Date: June 23, 1972

National Team: France (1994–06)

World Cups: 1998 (win), 2002, 2006

Pro Career: 1988–2006

Club Teams: Cannes (France), 1988–92; Bordeaux (France), 1992–96; Juventus (Italy), 1996–2001; Real Madrid (Spain), 2001–06

World Cup Honors: Golden Ball, 2006

World Player of the Year: 1998, 2000, 2003

European Player of the Year: 1998

RONALDO

Ronaldo had won a World Cup as a 17-year-old backup in 1994. He was at the top of the professional game for years. But in 2002, the striker cemented his place among the all-time greats.

Brazil played in six games leading up to the 2002 final. Ronaldo tallied six goals along the way, scoring in five of the six games. Then in the final against Germany, he scored two more times. One was off a rebound. The other was a low snipe from the top of the penalty box. Brazil won the game 2–0 to claim its fifth World Cup. Ronaldo's eight goals led the tournament.

Ronaldo had a unique ability to finish scoring opportunities. His combination of power and masterful ball control allowed him to drive past defenders. He had a rocket for a shot, if needed. Often, though, his positioning meant he just needed a well-placed shot. And he had that too.

Ronaldo shows off his 1997 World Player of the Year trophy.

Ronaldo came into the 1998 World Cup as the two-time World Player of the Year. He then scored four goals en route to the finals. But a mysterious ailment struck him the night before the final. Ronaldo was a shell of himself in a 3–0 loss to France.

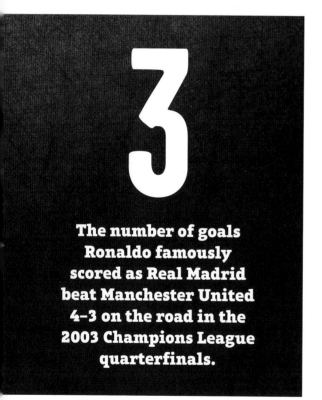

3

The number of goals Ronaldo famously scored as Real Madrid beat Manchester United 4–3 on the road in the 2003 Champions League quarterfinals.

The 2002 World Cup win helped make up for that disappointment. Brazil fell short of another win in Ronaldo's final World Cup, in 2006. But his breakaway goal in the round of 16 was historic. It was his record fifteenth goal in World Cup play.

Injuries and poor fitness limited Ronaldo at times in his career. But he played for some of the biggest club teams in the world. His three World Player of the Year Awards are tied with Zinedine Zidane for the second most all time. And for Brazil, Ronaldo is in a class with the very best.

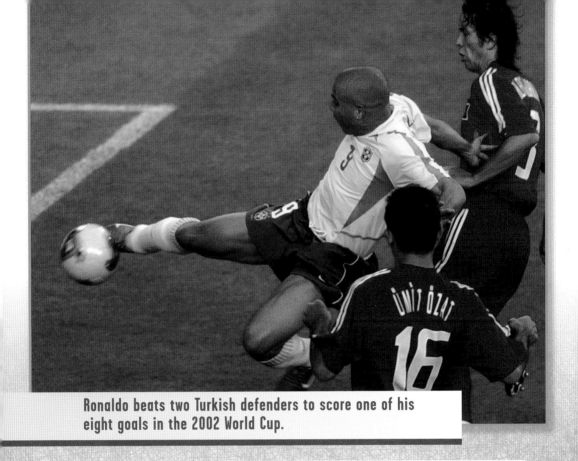

Ronaldo beats two Turkish defenders to score one of his eight goals in the 2002 World Cup.

RONALDO LUIS NAZARIO DE LIMA

Position: Forward

Hometown: Rio de Janeiro, Brazil

Birth Date: September 22, 1976

National Team: Brazil (1994–2011)

World Cups: 1994 (win), 1998, 2002 (win), 2006

Pro Career: 1993–2011

Club Teams: Cruzeiro (Brazil), 1993–94; PSV Eindhoven (Netherlands), 1994–96; Barcelona (Spain), 1996–97; Inter Milan (Italy), 1997–2002; Real Madrid (Spain), 2002–07; AC Milan (Italy), 2007–08; Corinthians (Brazil) 2009–11

World Cup Honors: Golden Ball, 1998; Silver Ball, 2002

World Player of the Year: 1996, 1997, 2002

49

ABBY WAMBACH

Abby Wambach grew up watching Mia Hamm score goals. By the early 2000s, Wambach was scoring goals alongside Hamm for the Washington Freedom and the US national team. They formed the most lethal scoring duo in women's soccer.

In 2004, Hamm and Wambach lined up together at the Olympics. It would be the last major tournament for Hamm and four other core members of the US team. So they were desperate to win. But through 112 minutes in the gold-medal game, the United States and Brazil remained tied 1–1. That is when the 24-year-old Wambach met the ball off a corner kick. It bounced off her head, hit a Brazilian defender, and ended up in the goal.

Wambach's score secured a 2–1 victory and a gold medal for the United States. It was also the perfect transition from one generation to the next.

Abby Wambach celebrates after her clutch goal against Brazil in the 2011 Women's World Cup quarterfinals.

Wambach can score with her head or her feet. She can score in friendlies or major tournaments. And she can score in bunches. Her biggest goal was in the 2011 Women's World Cup quarterfinals. Less than two minutes remained in extra time. Brazil led 2–1. That is when a long-range, desperate cross found Wambach at the far post. Her header goal sent the game to a shootout. The United States won the game and went on to finish second in the tournament.

On June 21, 2013, Wambach scored four goals in one game. That gave her 160 international goals for her career. More importantly, it moved her past Hamm's previous record of 158. And at age 33 in 2014, Wambach was still going strong. Like Hamm, she had become the role model for the next generation of young soccer players.

31

The number of goals Abby Wambach scored in international play in 2004. That was her highest total through 2013.

Abby Wambach, *center*, heads a goal past two French defenders in the 2011 Women's World Cup semifinals.

ABBY WAMBACH

Position: Forward

Hometown: Rochester, New York

Birth Date: June 2, 1980

National Team: United States (2001–)

Women's World Cups: 2003, 2007, 2011

Olympic Games: 2004 (gold), 2012 (gold)

Pro Career: 2002–

Club Teams: Washington Freedom (USA), 2002–03, 2009–10; magicJack (USA), 2011; Western New York Flash (USA), 2013–

World Cup Honors: Silver Ball, 2011

World Player of the Year: 2012

MARTA

A Brazilian known by just one name received the ball. It was not Pelé, Ronaldo, or any of the other famous Brazilian male soccer players. It was Marta—the best women's player in the world.

Marta tapped the ball into the air. Then with her left foot, she flicked the ball behind her. The ball rolled to one side of a US defender; Marta went around the other side. Another US defender closed in on Marta at the left edge of the penalty box. But the Brazilian star faked to the outside and cut back inside. Drilling the close-range shot into the net was the easy part.

Brazil won that 2007 Women's World Cup semifinal game 4–0. The goal was one of Marta's tournament-leading seven. Afterward, she won the Golden Ball as the tournament's top player.

Marta celebrates a goal against Team USA in the 2011 Women's World Cup quarterfinals.

Brazil has a rich tradition in men's soccer. The country had few opportunities for females, though. So Marta grew up playing with the boys on the streets of Dois Riachos. At age 14, Marta finally joined a girls' team in Rio de Janeiro. But her development really took off three years later.

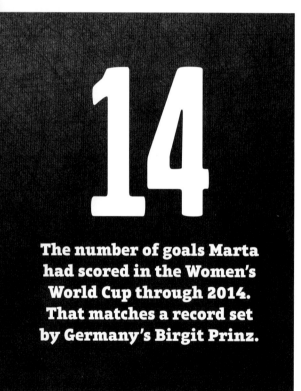

14

The number of goals Marta had scored in the Women's World Cup through 2014. That matches a record set by Germany's Birgit Prinz.

In 2004 at age 17, Marta joined a professional women's team in Sweden. She dazzled fans with her dribbling skills and goal-scoring ability. And in 2006, she won her first Women's World Player of the Year Award. Then she won the award again in each of the next four years.

Often called "Pelé with skirts," Marta became the biggest star in women's soccer. She helped make Brazil a powerful team too. Through 2014, she had played in three Women's World Cups and three Olympic Games. Behind Marta, Brazil was runner-up at the 2007 World Cup and the 2004 and 2008 Olympics.

Marta is mobbed by her teammates after scoring one of her seven goals in the 2007 Women's World Cup.

MARTA VIEIRA DA SILVA

Position: Forward and midfielder

Hometown: Dois Riachos, Brazil

Birth Date: February 19, 1986

National Team: Brazil (2003–)

Women's World Cups: 2003, 2007, 2011

Olympic Games: 2004, 2008, 2012

Pro Career: 2004–

Club Teams: Umea IK (Sweden), 2004–2008; Los Angeles Sol (USA), 2009; FC Gold Pride (USA), 2010; Western New York Flash (USA), 2011; Tyreso FF (Sweden), 2014–

World Cup Honors: Golden Ball, 2007

World Player of the Year: 2006, 2007, 2008, 2009, 2010

LIONEL MESSI

Lionel Messi had proven to be the world's best player for his club team, Barcelona. Though just 27 years old, the forward from Argentina had already won four World Player of the Year awards and three Champions League titles.

Messi's record for Argentina was less sterling, though. Then in the 2014 World Cup, he finally came through. Argentina was tied 0–0 with Iran in the 91st minute. Messi beat a defender, then shot from outside the penalty box. The ball curved around another defender and back inside the far post. It was one of four goals he scored in the tournament. Messi won the Golden Ball and led Argentina to the final.

Argentina fans long had a complex relationship with Messi. He was born in that country. But when his club team refused to pay for medical treatment, the 13-year-old chose to join Barcelona, which did pay.

Lionel Messi led Argentina to a second-place finish at the 2014 World Cup.

The move paid off for the Spanish team. Though just 5-foot-6 and 148 pounds, Messi proved to be one of the best offensive players of all time. He made his Barcelona debut in 2004 at age 17. He played a key role in the team's 2006, 2009, and 2011 Champions League wins. Although he was injured for the 2006 final, Messi scored in the 2009 and 2011 finals. Barcelona also won six Spanish league titles and two Copa del Rey titles after Messi made his debut.

Yet for Argentina, Messi had failed to impress in the 2006 and 2010 World Cups. That changed in 2014. Argentina's Messi played like Barcelona's Messi. With bursts of speed and amazing ball control, Messi made world-class defenders look like beginners. He scored goals and set up teammates for more. Though he did not match countryman Diego Maradona by leading the team to victory, Messi left no doubt that he was indeed one of the all-time greats.

24

Lionel Messi's age when he became the all-time top scorer at Barcelona. He scored his record-breaking 233rd goal in March 2012.

Lionel Messi has been a star for Barcelona for more than a decade.

LIONEL MESSI

Position: Forward
Hometown: Rosario, Argentina
Birth Date: June 24, 1987
National Team: Argentina (2005–)
World Cups: 2006, 2010, 2014
Pro Career: 2002–
Club Team: Barcelona (Spain), 2004–
World Cup Honors: Golden Ball, 2014
World Player of the Year: 2009, 2010, 2011, 2012

HONORABLE MENTIONS

Michelle Akers (USA) – The first superstar in women's soccer, Akers shared Female Player of the Century honors in 2000.

David Beckham (England) – Perhaps the most famous soccer player of all time, Beckham was a world-class midfielder for Manchester United and Real Madrid. He was feared for his lethal free kicks. Beckham finished his career with the Los Angeles Galaxy, helping grow the sport in the United States.

Cafu (Brazil) – The sturdy right back played in four World Cups for Brazil, winning the tournament in 1994 and again as captain in 2002. He also won the 2007 Champions League title with AC Milan.

Bobby Charlton (England) – Charlton and teammate Bobby Moore led the way as England won the 1966 World Cup on home soil. Charlton, a high-scoring attacking midfielder who also played for Manchester United, became a legend in England.

Eusébio (Portugal) – "The Black Panther" shined at the 1966 World Cup with nine goals. A longtime striker for Benfica in his home country, Eusébio was the 1965 European Player of the Year.

Ferenc Puskás (Hungary) – Puskás was a prolific goal scorer who played with Alfredo di Stéfano at Real Madrid in the 1950s and 1960s. His Hungarian national team, known as the "Magical Magyars," might have been the best to never win a World Cup.

Garrincha (Brazil) – With Pelé injured, the winger led the way as Brazil won its second World Cup in 1962. Garrincha, who also played on the winning 1958 team, was known for his creativity.

Gerd Müller (West Germany) – A true marksman, Müller scored 365 goals in 427 league games for Bayern Munich and 68 goals in 62 games for West Germany, including four in the winning 1974 World Cup campaign.

Cristiano Ronaldo (Portugal) – Known for his amazing athleticism and ball control, Ronaldo was the 2008 and 2013 World Player of the Year.

GLOSSARY

caps
Matches played with a national team.

charismatic
Appealing or likeable.

extra time
Two 15-minute periods added to a game if the score remains tied after regulation.

friendly
A soccer game that is not part of an official competition or league.

group stage
A round-robin competition in which four teams play each other to determine which two teams advance to the knockout round.

knockout round
The single-elimination round of a tournament.

shootout
A method of deciding a game if the score remains tied through regulation and extra time.

transfer fee
The price a club team pays to obtain the rights to a player. In world soccer, transfers are more common than outright player trades.

volley
A kick to an airborne ball.

FOR MORE INFORMATION

Further Readings

McDougall, Chrös. *Soccer*. Minneapolis, MN: Abdo Publishing, 2012.

Monnig, Alex. *The World Cup*. Minneapolis, MN: Abdo Publishing, 2012.

Trusdell, Brian. *Pelé: Soccer Star and Ambassador*. Minneapolis, MN: Abdo Publishing, 2014.

Websites

To learn more about Sports' Best Ever, visit **booklinks.abdopublishing.com**. These links are routinely monitored and updated to provide the most current information available.

INDEX

ABOUT THE AUTHOR

Chrös McDougall is a reporter, author, and editor who focuses on soccer, Olympic sports, and history. He began following soccer closely before the 1998 World Cup and frequently beat his brother in soccer video games growing up. He covered English soccer as an intern with the Associated Press' London bureau in 2007, including the first match at the new Wembley Stadium. McDougall lives with his wife in the Twin Cities of Minneapolis and St. Paul, Minnesota.